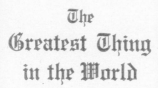

The Greatest Thing in the World

By
Henry Drummond

Philadelphia
Henry Altemus Company

THOUGH I speak with the tongues of men and of angels, and have not charity, I am become *as* sounding brass, or a tinkling cymbal.

2 And though I have *the gift of* prophecy, and understand all mysteries, and all knowledge; and though I have all faith, so that I could remove mountains, and have not charity, I am nothing.

3 And though I bestow all my goods to feed *the poor*, and though I give my body to be burned, and have not charity, it profiteth me nothing.

4 Charity suffereth long, *and* is kind; charity envieth not; charity vaunteth not itself, is not puffed up.

5 Doth not behave itself unseemly, seeketh not her own, is not easily provoked, thinketh no evil;

6 Rejoiceth not in iniquity, but rejoiceth in the truth;

7 Beareth all things, believeth all things, hopeth all things, endureth all things.

8 Charity never faileth: but whether *there be* prophecies, they shall fail; whether *there be* tongues, they shall cease; whether *there be* knowledge, it shall vanish away.

9 For we know in part, and we prophesy in part.

10 But when that which is perfect is come, then that which is in part shall be done away.

11 When I was a child, I spake as a child, I understood as a child, I thought as a child; but when I became a man, I put away childish things.

12 For now we see through a glass, darkly; but then face to face: now I know in part; but then shall I know even as also I am known.

13 And now abideth faith, hope, charity, these three; but the greatest of these *is* charity.

THE GREATEST THING

IN

THE WORLD

THE GREATEST THING
IN THE WORLD.

EVERY one has asked himself the great question of antiquity as of the modern world: What is the *summum bonum* — the supreme good? You have life before you. Once only you can live it. What is the noblest object of desire, the supreme gift to covet?

We have been accustomed to be told that the greatest thing in the religious world is Faith. That great word has been the key-note for centuries of the popular religion; and we have easily learned to look upon it as the greatest thing in the world. Well, we are wrong. If we have been told that, we may miss the mark. I have taken you, in the chapter which I have just read, to Christianity at his source; and there we have seen, "The greatest of these is love." It is not an oversight. Paul was speaking of faith just a moment before. He says, "If I have all faith, so that I can remove mountains, and have not love, I am nothing." So far from forgetting he deliberately contrasts them, "Now abideth, Faith, Hope, Love," and without a moment's hesitation the decision falls, "The greatest of these is Love."

And it is not prejudice. A man is apt to recommend to others his own strong point. Love was not Paul's strong point. The observing student can detect a beautiful tenderness growing and ripening all through his character as Paul gets old; but the hand that wrote, " The greatest of these is love," when we meet it first, is stained with blood.

Nor is this letter to the Corinthians peculiar in singling out love as the *summum bonum*. The masterpieces of Christianity are agreed about it. Peter says, " Above all things have fervent love among yourselves." *Above all things*. And John goes farther, " God is love." And you remember

13

the profound remark which Paul makes elsewhere, " Love is the fulfilling of the law." Did you ever think what he meant by that ? In those days men were working the passage to Heaven by keeping the Ten Commandments, and the hundred and ten other commandments which they had manufactured out of them. Christ said, I will show you a more simple way. If you do one thing, you will do these hundred and ten things, without ever thinking about them. If you love, you will unconsciously fulfill the whole law. And you can readily see for yourselves how that must be so. Take any of the commandments. " Thou shalt have no other gods before Me."

14

If a man love God, you will not re-
quire to tell him that. Love is the
fulfilling of that law. "Take not His
name in vain." Would he ever dream
of taking His name in vain if he loved
him? "Remember the Sabbath day
to keep it holy." Would he not be too
glad to have one day in seven to dedi-
cate more exclusively to the object of
his affection? Love would fulfill all
these laws regarding God. And so,
if he loved Man, you would never
think of telling him to honor his father
and mother. He could not do anything else. It would be preposterous
to tell him not to kill. You could only
insult him if you suggested that he
should not steal — how could he steal

from those he loved? It would be
superfluous to beg him not to bear false
witness against his neighbor. If he
loved him it would be the last thing he
would do. And you would never
dream of urging him not to covet what
his neighbors had. He would rather
they possessed it than himself. In
this way "Love is the fulfilling of the
law." It is the rule for fulfilling all
rules, the new commandment for keeping all the old commandments, Christ's
one secret of the Christian life.

Now Paul has learned that; and in
this noble eulogy he has given us the
most wonderful and original account
extant of the *summum bonum*. We
may divide it into three parts. In the

beginning of the short chapter, we have Love *contrasted;* in the heart of it, we have Love *analyzed;* toward the end, we have Love *defended* as the supreme gift.

THE CONTRAST.

PAUL begins by contrasting Love
with other things that men in
those days thought much of. I shall
not attempt to go over these things in
detail. Their inferiority is already
obvious.

He contrasts it with eloquence. And
what a noble gift it is, the power of
playing upon the souls and wills of
men, and rousing them to lofty pur-
poses and holy deeds. Paul says, "If
I speak with the tongues of men and
of angels, and have not love, I am

become as sounding brass, or a tinkling cymbal." And we all know
why. We have all felt the brazenness
of words without emotion, the hollow-
ness, the unaccountable unpersuasive-
ness, of eloquence behind which lies
no Love.

He contrasts it with prophecy. He
contrasts it with mysteries. He contrasts it with faith. He contrasts it
with charity. Why is Love greater
than faith? Because the end is greater
than the means. And why is it greater
than charity? Because the whole is
greater than the part. Love is greater
than faith, because the end is greater
than the means. What is the use of
having faith? It is to connect the soul

with God. And what is the object of connecting man with God? That he may become like God. But God is Love. Hence Faith, the means, is in order to Love, the end. Love, therefore, obviously is greater than faith. It is greater than charity, again, because the whole is greater than a part. Charity is only a little bit of Love, one of the innumerable avenues of Love, and there may even be, and there is, a great deal of charity without Love. It is a very easy thing to toss a copper to a beggar on the street; it is generally an easier thing than not to do it. Yet Love is just as often in the withholding. We purchase relief from the sympathetic feelings roused by the spectacle of misery, at the copper's cost. It is too cheap — too cheap for us, and often too dear for the beggar. If we really loved him we would either do more for him, or less.

Then Paul contrasts it with sacrifice and martyrdom. And I beg the little band of would-be missionaries — and I have the honor to call some of you by this name for the first time — to remember that though you give your bodies to be burned, and have not Love, it profits nothing — nothing! You can take nothing greater to the heathen world than the impress and reflection of the Love of God upon your own character. That is the universal language. It will take you years to speak in Chinese, or in the dialects of India. From the day you land, that language of Love, understood by all, will be pouring forth its unconscious eloquence. It is the man who is the missionary, it is not his words. His character is his message. In the heart of Africa, among the great Lakes, I have come across black men and women who remembered the only white man they ever saw before — David Livingstone; and as you cross his footsteps in that dark continent, men's faces light up as they speak of the kind doctor who passed there years ago. They could not understand him; but they felt the love that

beat in his heart. Take into your
new sphere of labor, where you also
mean to lay down your life, that simple charm, and your lifework must
succeed. You can take nothing
greater, you need take nothing less.
It is not worth while going if you take
anything less. You may take every
accomplishment; you may be braced
for every sacrifice; but if you give
your body to be burned, and have not
Love, it will profit you and the cause
of Christ *nothing*.

THE ANALYSIS.

AFTER contrasting Love with these things, Paul, in three verses, very short, gives us an amazing analysis of what this supreme thing is. I ask you to look at it. It is a compound thing, he tells us. It is like light. As you have seen a man of science take a beam of light and pass it through a crystal prism, as you have seen it come out on the other side of the prism broken up into its component colors — red, and blue, and yellow, and violet, and orange, and all the colors of the rainbow — so Paul passes this thing, Love, through the magnificent prism of his inspired intellect, and it comes out on the other side broken up into its elements. And in these few words we have what one might call the Spectrum of Love, the analysis of Love. Will you observe what its elements are? Will you notice that they have common names; that they are virtues which we hear about every day; that they are things which can be practiced by every man in every place in life; and how, by a multitude of small things and ordinary virtues, the supreme thing, the *summum bonum*, is made up?

The Spectrum of Love has nine ingredients:

Patience . . .	"Love suffereth long."
Kindness . . .	"And is kind."
Generosity . .	"Love envieth not."
Humility . . .	"Love vaunteth not itself, is not puffed up."
Courtesy . . .	"Doth not behave itself unseemly."
Unselfishness .	"Seeketh not her own."
Good Temper .	"Is not easily provoked."
Guilelessness . .	"Thinketh no evil."
Sincerity . . .	"Rejoiceth not in iniquity, but rejoiceth in the truth."

Patience; kindness; generosity; humility; courtesy; unselfishness; good temper; guilelessness; sincerity —these make up the supreme gift, the

stature of the perfect man. You will
observe that all are in relation to men,
in relation to life, in relation to the
known to-day and the near to-morrow,
and not to the unknown eternity. We
hear much of love to God; Christ
spoke much of love to man. We
make a great deal of peace with
heaven; Christ made much of peace
on earth. Religion is not a strange or
added thing, but the inspiration of the
secular life, the breathing of an eternal
spirit through this temporal world.
The supreme thing, in short, is not a
thing at all, but the giving of a further
finish to the multitudinous words and
acts which make up the sum of every
common day.

There is no time to do more than make a passing note upon each of these ingredients. Love is *Patience*. This is the normal attitude of Love; Love passive, Love waiting to begin; not in a hurry; calm; ready to do its work when the summons comes, but meantime wearing the ornament of a meek and quiet spirit. Love suffers long; beareth all things; believeth all things; hopeth all things. For Love understands, and therefore waits.

Kindness. Love active. Have you ever noticed how much of Christ's life was spent in doing kind things — in *merely* doing kind things? Run over it with that in view, and you will find that He spent a great proportion of His time simply in making people happy, in doing good turns to people. There is only one thing greater than happiness in the world, and that is holiness; and it is not in our keeping; but what God *has* put in our power is the happiness of those about us, and that is largely to be secured by our being kind to them.

"The greatest thing," says some one, "a man can do for his Heavenly Father is to be kind to some of His other children." I wonder why it is that we are not all kinder than we are? How much the world needs it. How easily it is done. How instantaneously it acts. How infallibly it is remembered. How superabundantly it pays itself back — for there is no debtor in the world so honorable, so superbly honorable, as Love. "Love never faileth." Love is success, Love is happiness, Love is life. "Love I say," with Browning, "is energy of Life."

"For life, with all it yields of joy or woe
And hope and fear,
Is just our chance o' the prize of learning love, —
How love might be, hath been indeed, and is."

Where Love is, God is. He that dwelleth in Love dwelleth in God. God is Love. Therefore *love*. Without distinction, without calculation, without procrastination, love. Lavish it upon the poor, where it is very easy; especially upon the rich, who often need it most; most of all upon our equals, where it is very difficult, and for whom perhaps we each do least of all. There is a difference between *trying to please* and *giving pleasure*. Give pleasure. Lose no chance of giving pleasure. For that is the ceaseless and anonymous triumph of a truly loving spirit. "I shall pass through this world but once. Any good thing therefore that I can do, or any kindness that I can show to any human being, let me do it now. Let me not defer it or neglect it, for I shall not pass this way again."

Generosity. "Love envieth not." This is love in competition with others.

Whenever you attempt a good work you will find other men doing the same kind of work, and probably doing it better. Envy them not. Envy is a feeling of ill-will to those who are in the same line as ourselves, a spirit of covetousness and detraction. How little Christian work even is a protection against un-Christian feeling. That most despicable of all the unworthy moods which cloud a Christian's soul assuredly waits for us on the threshold of every work, unless we are fortified with this grace of magnanimity. Only one thing truly need the Christian envy, the large, rich, generous soul which " envieth not."

And then, after having learned all

that, you have to learn this further
thing, *Humility* — to put a seal upon
your lips and forget what you have
done. After you have been kind, after
Love has stolen forth into the world
and done its beautiful work, go back
into the shade again and say nothing
about it. Love hides even from itself.
Love waives even self-satisfaction.
"Love vaunteth not itself, is not puffed
up."

The fifth ingredient is a somewhat
strange one to find in this *summum
bonum: Courtesy*. This is Love in
society, Love in relation to etiquette.
"Love does not behave itself unseemly." Politeness has been defined as
love in trifles. Courtesy is said to be

love in little things. And the one
secret of politeness is to love. Love
cannot behave itself unseemly. You
can put the most untutored persons
into the highest society, and if they
have a reservoir of Love in their heart
they will not behave themselves unseemly. They simply cannot do it.
Carlisle said of Robert Burns that
there was no truer gentleman in Europe
than the ploughman-poet. It was
because he loved everything — the
mouse, and the daisy, and all the
things, great and small, that God had
made. So with this simple passport
he could mingle with any society, and
enter courts and palaces from his little
cottage on the banks of the Ayr. You

34

know the meaning of the word "gentleman." It means a gentle man — a man who does things gently with love. And that is the whole art and mystery of it. The gentle man cannot in the nature of things do an ungentle, an ungentlemanly thing. The ungentle soul, the inconsiderate, unsympathetic nature, cannot do anything else. "Love doth not behave itself unseemly."

Unselfishness. "Love seeketh not her own." Observe: Seeketh not even that which is her own. In Britain the Englishman is devoted, and rightly, to his rights. But there come times when a man may exercise even the higher right of giving up his rights.

35

Yet Paul does not summon us to give up our rights. Love strikes much deeper. It would have us not seek them at all, ignore them, eliminate the personal element altogether from our calculations. It is not hard to give up our rights. They are often external. The difficult thing is to give up ourselves. The more difficult thing still is not to seek things for ourselves at all. After we have sought them, bought them, won them, deserved them, we have taken the cream off them for ourselves already. Little cross then to give them up. But not to seek them, to look every man not on his own things, but on the things of others — *id opus est.* "Seekest thou great things for thyself," said the prophet; "*seek them not.*" Why? Because there is no greatness in *things*. Things cannot be great. The only greatness is unselfish love. Even self-denial in itself is nothing, is almost a mistake. Only a great purpose or a mightier love can justify the waste. It is more difficult, I have said, not to seek our own at all, than, having sought it, to give it up. I must take that back. It is only true of a partly selfish heart. Nothing is a hardship to Love, and nothing is hard. I believe that Christ's "yoke" is easy. Christ's yoke is just his way of taking life. And I believe it is an easier way than any other. I believe it is a happier way than any other. The most obvious lesson in Christ's teaching is that there is no happiness in having and getting anything, but only in giving. I repeat, *there is no happiness in having or in getting, but only in giving*. And half the world is on the wrong scent in pursuit of happiness. They think it consists in having and getting, and in being served by others. It consists in giving, and in serving others. He that would be great among you, said Christ, let him serve. He that would be happy, let him remember that there is but one way — it is more blessed, it is more happy, to give than to receive.

The next ingredient is a very re-

markable one: *Good temper.* "Love
is not easily provoked." Nothing could
be more striking than to find this
here. We are inclined to look upon
bad temper as a very harmless weakness. We speak of it as a mere in-
firmity of nature, a family failing, a
matter of temperament, not a thing to
take into very serious account in esti-
mating a man's character. And yet
here, right in the heart of this analysis
of love, it finds a place; and the Bible
again and again returns to condemn it
as one of the most destructive elements
in human nature.

The peculiarity of ill temper is that
it is the vice of the virtuous. It
is often the one blot on an otherwise

noble character. You know men who are all but perfect, and women who would be entirely perfect, but for an easily ruffled, quick-tempered, or "touchy" disposition. This compatibility of ill temper with high moral character is one of the strangest and saddest problems of ethics. The truth is there are two great classes of sins — sins of the *Body*, and sins of the *Disposition*. The Prodigal Son may be taken as a type of the first, the Elder Brother of the second. Now, society has no doubt whatever as to which of these is the worse. Its brand falls, without a challenge, upon the Prodigal. But are we right? We have no balance to weigh one another's sins, and

coarser and finer are but human words;
but faults in the higher nature may be
less venial than those in the lower,
and to the eye of Him who is Love, a
sin against Love may seem a hundred
times more base. No form of vice,
not worldliness, not greed of gold, not
drunkenness itself, does more to un-
Christianize society than evil temper.
For embittering life, for breaking up
communities, for destroying the most
sacred relationships, for devastating
homes, for withering up men and
women, for taking the bloom of child-
hood, in short, for sheer gratuitous
misery-producing power, this influence
stands alone. Look at the Elder
Brother, moral, hard-working, patient,

41

dutiful — let him get all credit for his
virtues — look at this man, this baby,
sulking outside his own father's door.
"He was angry," we read, "and
would not go in." Look at the effect
upon the father, upon the servants,
upon the happiness of the guests.
Judge of the effect upon the Prodigal
— and how many prodigals are kept
out of the Kingdom of God by the unlovely character of those who profess
to be inside? Analyze, as a study in
Temper, the thunder-cloud itself as it
gathers upon the Elder Brother's brow.
What is it made of? Jealousy, anger,
pride, uncharity, cruelty, self-right-
eousness, touchiness, doggedness, sul-
lenness — these are the ingredients of

this dark and loveless soul. In varying proportions, also, these are the ingredients of all ill temper. Judge if such sins of the disposition are not worse to live in, and for others to live with, than sins of the body. Did Christ indeed not answer the question Himself when He said, "I say unto you, that the publicans and the harlots go into the Kingdom of Heaven before you." There is really no place in Heaven for a disposition like this. A man with such a mood could only make Heaven miserable for all the people in it. Except, therefore, such a man be born again, he cannot, he simply *cannot*, enter the Kingdom of Heaven. For it is perfectly certain —

43

and you will not misunderstand me —
that to enter Heaven a man must take
it with him.

You will see then why Temper is
significant. It is not in what it is
alone, but in what it reveals. This
is why I take the liberty now of speaking of it with such unusual plainness.
It is a test for love, a symptom, a reve-
lation of an unloving nature at bottom.
It is the intermittent fever which be-
speaks unintermittent disease within;
the occasional bubble escaping to the
surface which betrays some rottenness
underneath; a sample of the most hid-
den products of the soul dropped in-
voluntarily when off one's guard; in a
word, the lightning form of a hundred

hideous and un-Christian sins. For a want of patience, a want of kindness, a want of generosity, a want of courtesy, a want of unselfishness, are all instantaneously symbolized in one flash of Temper.

Hence it is not enough to deal with the Temper. We must go to the source, and change the inmost nature, and the angry humors will die away of themselves. Souls are made sweet not by taking the acid fluids out, but by putting something in — a great Love, a new Spirit, the Spirit of Christ. Christ, the Spirit of Christ, interpenetrating ours, sweetens, purifies, transforms all. This only can eradicate what is wrong, work a chemical change, renovate and regenerate, and rehabilitate the inner man. Willpower does not change men. Time does not change men. Christ does. Therefore "Let that mind be in you which was also in Christ Jesus." Some of us have not much time to lose. Remember, once more, that this is a matter of life or death. I cannot help speaking urgently, for myself, for yourselves. "Whoso shall offend one of these little ones, which believe in me, it were better for him that a millstone were hanged about his neck, and that he were drowned in the depth of the sea." That is to say, it is the deliberate verdict of the Lord Jesus that it is better not to live than

not to love. *It is better not to live than not to love.*

Guilelessness and *Sincerity* may be dismissed almost without a word. Guilelessness is the grace for suspicious people. And the possession of it is the great secret of personal influence. You will find, if you think for a moment, that the people who influence you are people who believe in you. In an atmosphere of suspicion men shrivel up; but in that atmosphere they expand, and find encouragement and educative fellowship. It is a wonderful thing that here and there in this hard, uncharitable world there should still be left a few rare souls who think no evil. This is the great unworldli-

ness. Love "thinketh no evil," im-
putes no motive, sees the bright side,
puts the best construction on every
action. What a delightful state of
mind to live in! What a stimulus and
benediction even to meet with it for
a day! To be trusted is to be saved.
And if we try to influence or elevate
others, we shall soon see that success
is in proportion to their belief of our
belief in them. For the respect of
another is the first restoration of the
self-respect a man has lost; our ideal
of what he is becomes to him the hope
and pattern of what he may become.

"Love rejoiceth not in iniquity, but
rejoiceth in the truth." I have called
this *Sincerity* from the words rendered

in the Authorized Version by "rejoiceth in the truth." And, certainly,
were this the real translation, nothing
could be more just. For he who
loves will love Truth not less than
men. He will rejoice in the Truth —
rejoice not in what he has been taught
to believe; not in this Church's doc-
trine or in that; not in this ism or in
that ism; but "in *the Truth.*" He
will accept only what is real; he will
strive to get at facts; he will search
for *Truth* with a humble and unbiassed
mind, and cherish whatever he finds
at any sacrifice. But the more literal
translation of the Revised Version
calls for just such a sacrifice for
truth's sake here. For what Paul

really meant is, as we there read,
" Rejoiceth not in unrighteousness, but
rejoiceth with the truth," a quality
which probably no one English word
— and certainly not *Sincerity* — ade-
quately defines. It includes, perhaps
more strictly, the self-restraint which
refuses to make capital out of others'
faults; the charity which delights not
in exposing the weakness of others,
but "covereth all things;" the sincerity of purpose which endeavors to
see things as they are, and rejoices to
find them better than suspicion feared
or calumny denounced.

So much for the analysis of Love.
Now the business of our lives is to
have these things fitted into our char-

acters. That is the supreme work to which we need to address ourselves in this world, to learn Love. Is life not full of opportunities for learning Love? Every man and woman every day has a thousand of them. The world is not a playground; it is a schoolroom. Life is not a holiday, but an education. And the one eternal lesson for as all is *how better we can love*. What makes a man a good cricketer? Practice. What makes a man a good artist, a good sculptor, a good musician? Practice. What makes a man a good linguist, a good stenographer? Practice. What makes a man a good man? Practice. Nothing else. There is nothing capricious about religion.

We do not get the soul in different ways, under different laws, from those in which we get the body and the mind. If a man does not exercise his arm he develops no biceps muscle; and if a man does not exercise his soul, he requires no muscle in his soul, no strength of character, no vigor of moral fibre, nor beauty of spiritual growth. Love is not a thing of enthusiastic emotion. It is a rich, strong, manly, vigorous expression of the whole round Christian character — the Christlike nature in its fullest development. And the constituents of this great character are only to be built up by ceaseless practice.

What was Christ doing in the car-

penter's shop? Practicing. Though
perfect, we read that He *learned* obe-
dience, and grew in wisdom and in
favor with God. Do not quarrel therefore with your lot in life. Do not com-
plain of its neverceasing cares, its
petty environment, the vexations you
have to stand, the small and sordid
souls you have to live and work with.
Above all, do not resent temptation;
do not be perplexed because it seems
to thicken round you more and more,
and ceases neither for effort nor for
agony nor prayer. That is your practice. That is the practice which God
appoints you; and it is having its work
in making you patient, and humble,
and generous, and unselfish, and kind,

and courteous. Do not grudge the hand that is moulding the still too shapeless image within you. It is growing more beautiful, though you see it not, and every touch of temptation may add to its perfection. Therefore keep in the midst of life. Do not isolate yourself. Be among men, and among things, and among troubles, and difficulties, and obstacles. You remember Goethe's words: *Es bildet ein Talent sich in der Stille, Doch ein Charakter in dem Strom der Welt.* "Talent develops itself in solitude; character in the stream of life." Talent develops itself in solitude — the talent of prayer, of faith, of meditation, of seeing the unseen; character grows in the stream of the world's life. That chiefly is where men are to learn love.

How? Now, how? To make it easier, I have named a few of the elements of love. But these are only elements. Love itself can never be defined. Light is a something more than the sum of its ingredients — a glowing, dazzling, tremulous ether. And love is something more than all its elements — a palpitating, quivering, sensitive, living thing. By synthesis of all the colors, men can make whiteness, they cannot make light. By synthesis of all the virtues, men can make virtue, they cannot make love. How then are we to have this transcendent living whole conveyed into our souls? We brace our wills to secure it. We try to copy those who have it. We lay down rules about it. We watch. We pray. But these things alone will not bring love into our nature. Love is an *effect*. And only as we fulfill the right condition can we have the effect produced. Shall I tell you what the *cause* is?

If you turn to the Revised Version of the First Epistle of John you will find these words: "We love because He first loved us." "We love," not "We love *Him*." That is the way the old version has it, and it is quite wrong. "*We love* — because He first loved us." Look at that word "because." It is the *cause* of which I have

56

spoken. "*Because* He first loved us," the effect follows that we love, we love Him, we love all men. We cannot help it. Because He loved us, we love, we love everybody. Our heart is slowly changed. Contemplate the love of Christ, and you will love. Stand before that mirror, reflect Christ's character, and you will be changed into the same image from tenderness to tenderness. There is no other way. You cannot love to order. You can only look at the lovely object, and fall in love with it, and grow into likeness to it. And so look at this Perfect Character, this Perfect Life. Look at the great Sacrifice as He laid down Himself, all through life, and upon the Cross of Calvary; and you must love Him. And loving Him, you must become like Him. Love begets love. It is a process of induction. Put a piece of iron in the presence of an electrified body, and that piece of iron for a time becomes electrified. It is changed into a temporary magnet in the mere presence of a permanent magnet, and as long as you leave the two side by side, they are both magnets alike. Remain side by side with Him who loved us, and gave Himself for us, and you too will become a permanent magnet, a permanently attractive force; and like Him you will draw all men unto you, like Him you will be drawn unto all

men. That is the inevitable effect of
Love. Any man who fulfills that
cause must have that effect produced
in him. Try to give up the idea that
religion comes to us by chance, or by
mystery, or by caprice. It comes to
us by natural law, or by supernatural
law, for all law is Divine. Edward
Irving went to see a dying boy once,
and when he entered the room he just
put his hand on the sufferer's head, and
said, "My boy, God loves you," and
went away. And the boy started from
his bed, and called out to the people
in the house, "God loves me! God
loves me!" It changed that boy. The
sense that God loved him overpowered
him, melted him down, and began the

creating of a new heart in him. **And**
that is how the love of God melts down
the unlovely heart in man, and begets
in him the new creature, who is patient
and humble and gentle and unselfish.
And there is no other way to get it.
There is no mystery about it. **We**
love others, we love everybody, we
love our enemies, because He first
loved us.

THE DEFENCE.

NOW I have a closing sentence or two to add about Paul's reason for singling out love as the supreme possession. It is a very remarkable reason. In a single word it is this: *it lasts.* "Love," urges Paul, "never faileth." Then he begins again one of his marvelous lists of the great things of the day, and exposes them one by one. He runs over the things that men thought were going to last, and shows that they are all fleeting, temporary, passing away.

"Whether there be prophecies, they shall fail." It was the mother's ambition for her boy in those days that he should become a prophet. For hundreds of years God had never spoken by means of any prophet, and at that time the prophet was greater than the King. Men waited wistfully for another messenger to come, and hung upon his lips when he appeared as upon the very voice of God. Paul says, "Whether there be prophecies, they shall fail." This book is full of prophecies. One by one they have "failed;" that is, having been fulfilled their work is finished; they have nothing more to do now in the world except to feed a devout man's faith.

Then **Paul** talks about **tongues.**
That was another thing that was greatly
coveted. "Whether there be tongues,
they shall cease." As we all know,
many, many centuries have passed
since tongues have been known in this
world. They have ceased. Take it
in any sense you like. Take it, for
illustration merely, as languages in
general — a sense which was not in
Paul's mind at all, and which though
it cannot give us the specific lesson
will point the general truth. Consider
the words in which these chapters were
written — Greek. It has gone. Take
the Latin — the other great tongue
of those days. It ceased long ago.
Look at the Indian language. It is

ceasing. The language of Wales, of Ireland, of the Scottish Highlands is dying before our eyes. The most popular book in the English tongue at the present time, except the Bible, is one of Dickens's works, his *Pickwick Papers*. It is largely written in the language of London street-life; and experts assure us that in fifty years it will be unintelligible to the average English reader.

Then Paul goes farther, and with even greater boldness adds, "Whether there be knowledge, it shall vanish away." The wisdom of the ancients, where is it? It is wholly gone. A schoolboy to-day knows more than Sir Isaac Newton knew. His knowledge has vanished away. You put yesterday's newspaper in the fire. Its knowledge has vanished away. You buy the old editions of the great encyclopædias for a few pence. Their knowledge has vanished away. Look how the coach has been superseded by the use of steam. Look how electricity has superseded that, and swept a hundred almost new inventions into oblivion. One of the greatest living authorities, Sir William Thompson, said the other day, "The steam-engine is passing away." "Whether there be knowledge, it shall vanish away." At every workshop you will see, in the back yard, a heap of old iron, a few wheels, a few levers, a few cranks, broken and eaten with rust. Twenty years ago that was the pride of the city. Men flocked in from the country to see the great invention; now it is superseded, its day is done. And all the boasted science and philosophy of this day will soon be old. But yesterday, in the University of Edinburgh, the greatest figure in the faculty was Sir James Simpson, the discoverer of chloroform. The other day his successor and nephew, Professor Simpson, was asked by the librarian of the University to go to the library and pick out the books on his subject that were no longer needed. And his reply to the librarian was this: "Take every text-book that is more than ten years old, and put it down in the cellar." Sir James Simpson was a great authority only a few years ago: men came from all parts of the earth to consult him; and almost the whole teaching of that time is consigned by the science of to-day to oblivion. And in every branch of science it is the same. "Now we know in part. We see through a glass darkly."

Can you tell me anything that is going to last? Many things Paul did not condescend to name. He did not mention money, fortune, fame; but he picked out the great things of his time, the things the best men thought had something in them, and brushed them peremptorily aside. Paul had no charge against these things in themselves. All he said about them was that they would not last. They were great things, but not supreme things. There were things beyond them. What we are stretches past what we do, beyond what we possess. Many things that men denounce as sins are not sins; but they are temporary. And that is a favorite argument of the New Testament. John says of the world, not that it is wrong, but simply that it "passeth away." There is a great deal in the world that is delightful and beautiful; there is a great deal in it that is great and engrossing; but it will not last. All that is in the world, the lust of the eye, the lust of the flesh, and the pride of life, are but for a little while. Love not the world therefore. Nothing that it contains is worth the life and consecration of an immortal soul. The immortal soul must give itself to something that is immortal. And the only immortal things are these: "Now abideth faith, hope, love, but the greatest of these is love."

Some think the time may come when two of these three things will also pass away — faith into sight, hope into fruition. Paul does not say so. We know but little now about the conditions of the life that is to come. But what is certain is that Love must last. God, the Eternal God, is Love. Covet therefore that everlasting gift, that one thing which it is certain is going to stand, that one coinage which will be current in the Universe when all the other coinages of all the nations of the world shall be useless and unhonored. You will give yourselves to many things, give yourself first to Love. Hold things in their proportion. *Hold things in their proportion.* Let at least the first great object of our lives be to achieve the character defended in these words, the character — and it is the character of Christ — which is built round Love.

I have said this thing is eternal. Did you ever notice how continually John associates love and faith with eternal life? I was not told when I was a boy that "God so loved the world that He gave His only-begotten Son, that whosoever believeth in Him should have everlasting life." What I was told, I remember, was, that God so loved the world that, if I trusted in Him, I was to have a thing called peace, or I was to have rest, or I was to have joy, or I was to have safety. But I had to find out for myself that whosoever trusteth in Him — that is, whosoever loveth Him, for trust is only the avenue to Love — hath everlasting *life*. The Gospel offers a man life. Never offer men a thimbleful of Gospel. Do not offer them merely joy, or merely peace, or merely rest, or merely safety; tell them how Christ came to give men a more abundant life than they have, a life abundant in love, and therefore abundant in salvation for themselves, and large in enterprise for the alleviation and redemption of the world. Then only can the Gospel take hold of the whole of a man, body, soul, and spirit, and give to each part of his nature its exercise and reward. Many of the current Gospels are addressed only to a part of man's nature. They offer peace, not life; faith, not Love; justification, not regeneration. And men slip back again from such religion because it has never really held them. Their nature was not all in it. It offered no deeper and gladder life-current than the life that was lived before. Surely it stands to reason that only a fuller love can compete with the love of the world.

To love abundantly is to live abundantly, and to love forever is to live forever. Hence, eternal life is inextricably bound up with love. We want to live forever for the same reason that we want to live to-morrow. Why do you want to live to-morrow? It is because there is some one who loves you, and whom you want to see to-morrow, and be with, and love back. There is no other reason why we should live on than that we love and are beloved. It is when a man has no one to love him that he commits suicide. So long as he has friends, those who love him and whom he loves, he will live, because to live is to love. Be it but the love of a dog, it will keep him in life; but let that go and he has no contact with life, no reason to live. He dies by his own hand. Eternal life also is to know God, and God is love. This is Christ's own definition. Ponder it. "This is life eternal, that they might know Thee the only true God, and Jesus Christ whom Thou has sent." Love must be eternal. It is what God is. On the last analysis, then, love is life. Love never faileth, and life never faileth, so long as there is love. That is the

philosophy of what Paul is showing us;
the reason why in the nature of things
Love should be the supreme thing —
because it is going to last; because in
the nature of things it is an Eternal
Life. It is a thing that we are living now, not that we get when we die;
that we shall have a poor chance of
getting when we die unless we are
living now. No worse fate can befall
a man in this world than to live and
grow old alone, unloving, and unloved.
To be lost is to live in an unregenerate
condition, loveless and unloved; and
to be saved is to love; and he that
dwelleth in love dwelleth already in
God. For God is Love.

Now I have all but finished. How

many of you will join me in reading
this chapter once a week for the next
three months? A man did that once
and it changed his whole life. Will
you do it? It is for the greatest thing
in the world. You might begin by
reading it every day, especially the
verses which describe the perfect character. "Love suffereth long, and is
kind; love envieth not; love vaunteth
not itself." Get these ingredients into
your life. Then everything that you
do is eternal. It is worth doing. It
is worth giving time to. No man can
become a saint in his sleep; and to
fulfill the condition required demands
a certain amount of prayer and meditation and time, just as improvement

in any direction, bodily or mental, requires preparation and care. Address yourselves to that one thing; at any cost have this transcendent character exchanged for yours. You will find as you look back upon your life that the moments that stand out, the moments when you have really lived, are the moments when you have done things in a spirit of love. As memory scans the past, above and beyond all the transitory pleasures of life, there leap forward those supreme hours when you have been enabled to do unnoticed kindnesses to those round about you, things too trifling to speak about, but which you feel have entered into your eternal life. I have seen

77

almost all the beautiful things God has
made; I have enjoyed almost every
pleasure that he has planned for man;
and yet as I look back I see standing
out above all the life that has gone
four or five short experiences when the
love of God reflected itself in some
poor imitation, some small act of love
of mine, and these seem to be the
things which alone of all one's life
abide. Everything else in all our
lives is transitory. Every other good
is visionary. But the acts of love
which no man knows about, or can
ever know about — they never fail.

In the Book of Matthew, where the
Judgment Day is depicted for us in
the imagery of One seated upon a

throne and dividing the sheep from the goats, the test of a man then is not, "How have I believed?" but "How have I loved?" The test of religion, the final test of religion, is not religiousness, but Love. I say the final test of religion at that great Day is not religiousness, but Love; not what I have done, not what I have believed, not what I have achieved, but how I have discharged the common charities of life. Sins of commission in that awful indictment are not even referred to. By what we have not done, *by sins of omission*, we are judged. It could not be otherwise. For the withholding of love is the negation of the spirit of Christ, the proof that we

never knew Him, that for us He lived
in vain. It means that He suggested
nothing in all our thoughts, that He
inspired nothing in all our lives, that
we were not once near enough to Him
to be seized with the spell of His com-
passion for the world. It means that —

"I lived for myself, I thought for myself,
  For myself, and none beside —
Just as if Jesus had never lived,
  As if He had never died."

It is the Son of *Man* before whom
the nations of the world shall be
gathered. It is in the presence of
Humanity that we shall be charged.
And the spectacle itself, the mere
sight of it, will silently judge each
one. Those will be there whom we

have met and helped; or there, the unpitied multitude whom we neglected or despised. No other witness need be summoned. No other charge than lovelessness shall be preferred. Be not deceived. The words which all of us shall one Day hear sound not of theology but of life, not of churches and saints but of the hungry and the poor, not of creeds and doctrines but of shelter and clothing, not of Bibles and prayer-books but of cups of cold water in the name of Christ. Thank God the Christianity of to-day is coming nearer the world's need. Live to help that on. Thank God men know better, by a hairsbreadth, what religion is, what God is, who Christ is, where

Christ is. Who is Christ? He who fed the hungry, clothed the naked, visited the sick. And where is Christ? Where? — whoso shall receive a little child in My name receiveth Me. And who are Christ's? Every one that loveth is born of God.